GLASS HEARTS
& BROKEN PROMISES

GLASS HEARTS
& BROKEN PROMISES

Andrews McMeel
PUBLISHING®

Andrews McMeel Publishing
a division of Andrews McMeel Universal
1130 Walnut Street, Kansas City, Missouri 64106

www.andrewsmcmeel.com

23 24 25 26 27 LAK 10 9 8 7 6 5 4 3 2 1

ISBN: 978-1-5248-9025-4

Library of Congress Control Number: 2023940277

Editor: Danys Mares
Art Director: Diane Marsh
Production Editor: Elizabeth A. Garcia
Production Manager: Shona Burns

Cover design and interior art by
Lisa-Marie Vecchio @lisadotdesign

ATTENTION: SCHOOLS AND BUSINESSES
Andrews McMeel books are available at quantity discounts with bulk purchase for educational, business, or sales promotional use. For information, please e-mail the Andrews McMeel Publishing Special Sales Department: sales@amuniversal.com.

dedication

for those who feel broken
and like they'll never be whole again

acknowledgments

when I think about all the people who have touched my
heart and have supported me throughout this journey,

I feel overwhelmed.

to my amazing parents, thank you for your unwavering

support. whatever I do and wherever I go, I promise to

always lead with love.

to Turner, the love of my life, thank you for being my light
in this world. I am grateful that everything in this life leads
me back home, to you.

to Tucker, my furry soulmate, we have grown so much

together. thank you for being my safe place.

to everyone else who has crossed my journey, thank you.

little flecks of your heart are embedded within this book.

contents

dear reader,

I used to wish for a love that was written in fairy tales and romance novels. I used to want someone to fight for me, like how a prince would fight for his princess. I would look for this love in every person who came into my life, and when they left, I was left questioning if I was ever good enough for it. This book is filled with the heartbreaks that line my heart, and within each scar, a lesson is embedded. I hope this book helps soothe your heartache and brings you one step closer to a healed version of yourself.

all my love,
kayla

before we begin
I'd like to tell you something
about me

I have a heart that's made of glass
not the kind of glass that's made
for weathering storms
or heroic events
not the kind of glass that
brings true love or
molds into a beautiful figurine
when lightning strikes
the ugly kind
the kind that breaks

the kind that takes an immeasurable
amount of time and effort to repair

it's full of colors that nobody likes

it's the kind that nobody wants

my heart is made of glass
much like what a promise is made of
and once broken
it can never be the same
it can never be renewed
only repaired

they say that you will experience
three kinds of love in your life
when I heard this
I didn't believe them
I had already experienced three times
that many by then
and it wasn't until I sat down
to write this book
and had outlined
all my heartaches
that I understood
they didn't mean the number
of hearts you would love
but the types of heartache
intertwined within that love

your first love is when you
love before you know
what love is
and your first heartbreak
happens when you break
your first heart
because you'll never
truly experience
another person's pain
unless you're staring
them in the face and
they can't bring
themselves to look
into the eyes they
once loved

your second love shows
you what love is
but doesn't stay
I think the other two
heartbreaks are embedded

within this love
one is folded neatly into
a box that you give out carelessly
you hand your heart
to someone
hoping that they
would keep it safe
and then they break it
and shatter it in ways
you never thought they could

another comes when you learn
that sometimes
loving someone means
letting them go and
watching them fall in love
with everything
and everyone
that isn't you

what they don't tell you
about your second heartbreak
is that it's the most pivotal
of them all
and sometimes you must
continuously experience it
to fully grasp the lesson at hand

you see the second heartbreak
leads you to your third love
finding the love
within you
and once you find that
life leads you to
finding true love

the love you get to keep

With every love you experience, you experience a heartache. Some will feel light, and others will make you question everything within life and yourself. Some will be easy to move on from and others you won't let go of for years. You will cry, and you will ache. But they come with a purpose, and it is your sole responsibility to heal through them. With everything we gain in this life, there's usually a loss that corresponds with it.

before you are ready
life will hand you heartbreak
and say, "let me teach you about you."

imagine someone wanting you
as much as you want them
embracing your flaws
teaching you to trust
I'd like to think that the heartbreaks
I experienced before you
were on purpose
leading me to a life
that would love me back
showing me that love
isn't supposed to hurt like that
and I can't help but think that
you're another heartbreak
just waiting to happen
another lesson
on how to let go
I don't want to lose you
but if I do
I really hope that
we were just two people
who had to lose each other
to find each other again

we were meant to happen
we were just never
meant to last

it hurts like hell when you know
that you have to let go of
someone and you can't
you feel like every move you make
is the wrong one
and every second chance you offer
ends up unwanted
so now you're just waiting
on the impossible to happen
waiting for them to change
waiting for them to notice
the love you're giving them

it hurts like hell when you know
that you have to let go of
the person you spent so long
trying to love

I'm not sure when it happened
when we went from friends
to something much more

maybe the chemistry
was always there
and that night alone
in your car was
the catalyst for
something that would
eventually tear us apart

I'm not sure how it happened
when our love became hatred

all I know is that right now
I'm sitting here
all alone
without my friend or a love
and a giant hole in my heart

please tell me that
just one small piece of you
loved me
like I loved you

on days like today
I'd give anything to pretend
that nothing went wrong
that you never left
that the night sky still shown
with stars that never dimmed
that the sun never hid away
and the birds kept singing

on days like today
I would give anything to be
back in your arms again

if forever was what you were wanting
I would have given it to you
I would have ripped open my chest
and taken out my heart
to stop time from moving
to stay in this moment with you

I'd soak up every smile
every tear
every kiss

and if this wasn't meant to last
and if the day came
and I'd have to be gone
you'd have my heart
to look back on

and it'd tell you
I loved you
with every beat

I wish I could let you go
without feeling 15
different kinds of hurt

sometimes all I want to do is cry
when the world feels heavy
and I feel defeated
crying is what takes it all away
they say it's healthy
to let go of what burdens us
but lately I feel like
I could drown in my tears
how does that make sense?
something that's supposed to free me
feels a lot like it's killing me

I want to believe them
when they say
time heals your heartbreak
but I can't
because I will always miss you
and I will always love you
and that heartbreak isn't going anywhere
but that's the thing with grief
time may ease the pain
but it's never truly gone
I think about what life would
have been like
if you'd been there for me more
showed up to the things that
were important to me
but I guess that's my closure

so, I close my eyes
and pray to God
that you're okay

and I think of you as someone
who would love me
who would be proud of me
no matter what

why did you come into my life
acting like you loved me
showing me something
I never had before
making me believe you cared
and then leave?

I don't want to live in a world
where we don't exist
a world where the person I once saw
a whole future with disappears
right in front of my eyes
all I want is to mean something to somebody
I want someone to choose me
over everything
and everyone else
choose me
because I will always choose you

if you were never meant to be my forever
tell my why sparks flew
when our souls collided
tell me why I saw our auras melt together
and the ripple in our destiny
tell me why your lips made me feel
shivers deep within my nerves

if you were never meant to be my forever
tell me why my heart memorized
every inch of you
every scar on your body
every line when you smiled
every paint stroke in your eyes

if you were never meant to be my forever
tell me why it's you I see when I close
my eyes at night

if you were never meant to be my forever
tell me why
and make me believe it

you knew I deserved more
and if I left
someone would give it to me
so, you made a home
in my bed at 2 am
you put your number on speed dial
and you made sure that it was
your voice I heard
when I needed help
you kept me hanging on
by a string
made me believe in every word
you would say
never giving me more
than what would keep me alive
you had me convinced
that you cared
without ever telling me
you loved me

we all make mistakes
your mistake was
believing I would never
stand up for myself
that I would always
come back to you

mine was thinking
this was love

I used to think that love could save you. That it could show you there's more to life than what you've been shown before. That if I gave you my all, it would fill up the empty spaces within you. That if I showed you my heart, it would make you forget all the hurt you've had to face. I wanted to show you what true love meant, but in the end, love couldn't save you, because I can't be the one who pulls your heart out of the hell it's stuck in. You're the one who must decide that love outweighs the risk of getting hurt.

the only wish I had
was for my heart to guide me
in the right direction
and look at me now
I'm broken

when I think of you
I think of all the things
I should have said
all the feelings
and sentences
and *I love you*s
that are still stuck on my tongue
that will forever be glued on my heart
I replay all our conversations
and wonder what I could have said
or done differently so that
this space between us
never existed
I think about all the times
I gave you the choice to choose me
and how every night was lonelier
than the last
am I too selfish for wanting this?
too selfish for wanting nothing more
than to be loved by you?

what's your favorite color?

blue, like the color of the sky
when the sun peaks over the horizon

blue, like the color of the clearest ocean

blue, like how snow reflects
off the tallest mountain

my favorite color is blue
like the color of his eyes
that kind of blue

if you can't love me right
please don't love me at all

we don't talk anymore
but sometimes I think
I can still hear you
in the wind
whispering through my hair
or while I'm sitting in the sun
soaking its rays into my skin
they tell me you love me
there is power in silence

there is pain in silence

I know that one day
I'll stop pretending that you never hurt me
I'll stop pretending that nothing bothers me
and confront the damage your heart did to mine
but today is not that day
and I like pretending
because with you gone
it's the only thing
that holds me at night

Kayla McCullough

I don't remember what you look like anymore
it hurts for me to admit that
I close my eyes
and I think I see you
I see your face and your hair
I see you sitting there
on your couch
reading a book
or watching a movie
but I don't actually see you
I don't see the lines on your face
or the curves in your body
are your freckles still there?
does your hair still curl when it's wet?
is there still a scar above your chest?

I'm beginning to believe that
life likes to play jokes on us
she gave us a memory
but we remember like goldfish
the things that are important to us
over time become blurred
she brings strangers
that come and turn your world upside down
they kiss you and they tell you they love you
and then fate lets them leave as lessons

I wish for the day
when I won't have to
rely on memories
to see you again

I remember feeling like a stranger
lying next to you in bed
because that's what we were
after all that time
strangers

I still find letters I never sent you
hidden beneath the tissues on my heart
they're filled with moments
I wanted to share with you
and questions that have gone unanswered
things I would forget
if I didn't write them down
did you hurt like me?
or did I consume the pain for the both of us?
do you still think about me?
or are the dreams I have one-sided?

we were meant to happen
we were meant to find each other
and fall in love
but like all storylines
full of shattered hearts
and broken promises
we were never meant to be

I thought that I missed you
thought that I missed the conversations
we used to have in bed
right before we would shut our eyes
I thought that I missed waking up beside you
kissing you and touching you
before you would leave every morning
I thought that I missed
the way you made me feel
because with you I felt everything
all at once
I thought that I missed that
and maybe I still do
but what I think I miss the most
is who I was when I was with you
how can I be that person again?

trust
something that comes too easily for a person
who opens their heart to strangers
because they know what it feels like
to peer in from the cold

I trusted you when I shouldn't have
I let you in to find comfort
in a bed that should've never
warmed your heart
I told you secrets
to calm your soul
and when you were no longer ill
from the torturous blizzards
that raged your mind
you violated me
you betrayed the friendship I gave you

and the betrayal from that night
has hung heavy in my heart
and has clouded my mind
so much so that when I cry
out in the middle of the night
it is only I who can hear the screams

at this point I think I've heard
all the goodbyes my heart can handle
I've been searching for love
in places that don't want me and
in hearts that can't love themselves
when does it end?
when does the time come for
my heart to finally be home?
they say that searching for love
is the same as searching for yourself
once you find you
you find love
I guess I'm still searching for me

it feels like I'll always be a little bit broken
and these scars will always remain
because one time is all that it takes
one lie
one kiss
one night
and the damage is done
the pieces of your heart are so fragmented
it feels impossible to put them back together

I watch as everyone around me willingly
gives their heart away
and I catch myself thinking
don't you know better?
hearts are breakable

what if there isn't enough love to keep you here?
what if I give you the entirety of my heart
lay it open on the table
and let you read between every break it's ever endured?
and then what if it all goes wrong?
it won't be easy picking up the pieces after you leave
and maybe it isn't supposed to be
but I'd be lying if I said I wouldn't miss you
so, would it be worth it?
falling in love with you?

I struggle with the idea of how replaceable
I am to some people
that to some people
I'm nothing more than a lesson
or a distant memory
of how a friendship used to be
or how a stranger turned into a lover
and how that lover is now a stranger once more
I struggle with the idea that once
I'm happy with life
life somehow takes that happiness away
and I'm alone again
I overthink
and it destroys me inside

lately I've been feeling like
I'm here but I'm not
like life is moving way too fast
and I can't catch up
like people love me for a second
and the next they don't
it feels like I wasn't made
to exist in this world
like I was made to exist anywhere
but here

I know that I overthink
and that my mind
is filled with today's anxieties
and tomorrow's worries
I know that I overlove
and that my heart
is full of today's grief
and tomorrow's hope
I know that I can
be insecure sometimes
and not want to be seen
I know that all of these things
make me
me
but my mind rages
war on my heart
they explode
and they both
tear me apart

but trust me
if I love you
I will think of you often
I will give you my whole heart
and I will make you feel
like you are never just an option

I think too much about
why good things have to end
why people have to leave
and why hearts have to break
I care too much about
what people think of me
if they think I look pretty
if I'm wearing clothes that are trendy
and if I'm saying the right things
I think and care too much about
how others feel because
I've spent a lifetime
not having anyone care about me

I can't wear this dress tonight
not because I don't like it
it's beautiful
but because
it's the color of his eyes
the same shade of blue
that's at the bottom of
the clearest ocean
accompanied by flecks of green
indicating that even beauty grows
in the most unexpected places
if I wear this tonight will people think
I'm not over him?

I can't wear this dress tonight
not because it doesn't look good on me
but because
what if it looks too good on me?
what if it hugs me in places
that make people stare?
they'll look at me and think I like it
the attention
the validation
but when their eyes move toward me
I shiver
I hate the attention
but if they see this dress
they'll think I'm a liar

I hang the dress back up
making sure its new home is
in the far back of my closet

sometimes I think if I distance myself
from the things that matter most
they won't matter that much anymore

Kayla McCullough

I overthink my past
and my future
my decisions
and my options
the things I've said
and the things I've done
and to make it worse
I allow myself to indulge
in what-ifs and worst-case scenarios
I create problems for myself
that aren't even real

today's peace is tomorrow's grief

what I've learned is that
things are rarely as bad
as what we expected them to be

it's hard for me to talk to others
to open up and think for one second
that I could have a friend
because all that friends do
is tell secrets
and then spill them
it's safer for me to be by myself

you feel too deeply
you think too much
even when you
feel or think
about nothing
it engulfs you

we don't simply let things go
because if we dig deeper
and aim to understand the meaning behind
every little thing that went wrong
we would be able to change the outcome
~overthinking

I think I've been left alone with my thoughts
and feelings for far too long
because lately everything is starting to make sense
people leave my life because I push them away
my heart breaks because I've never built its foundation
my mind races because I like control over situations
I'm not their first choice
because I'm not my first choice either
maybe life isn't out to get me
and God doesn't hate me
maybe I've just been sabotaging myself

I'm not sure if this will ever stop hurting
if my tears will ever stop flowing
or if I'll ever stop waking up at 2 am searching
for your body that should be next to mine

the biggest lie your heart ever told
was that it loved mine
tell it to me again

my heart has a way of falling in love
with the person who's going to do
the most damage
I think it likes being broken

I'm not sure how I managed to convince myself
that this would never hurt
that I'd be able to wash you off my body and
fold you nicely into a drawer
until your name didn't hurt anymore
looks like I'm more naive than I thought

while I was loving you
I was losing me
while I was holding on to you
you were letting me go
while I was fighting
to keep everything together
you didn't care about staying
and you decided to leave

you broke my heart
but my heart aches for me
because

I'm the girl
who doesn't know how
to let go
the girl who loses herself
loving everybody else

I'm the girl who loves to a fault

I guess a part of me knew
that we were never going to make it
that something was always going to stay
broken between us
I think I had seen it in your eyes one night
when you looked at me
I knew deep down that something
was never going to be the same
and it made me hold on even tighter
it was one of the most painful goodbyes because
even though we had just started
to get to know each other
I knew it was really over
you were gone and
you weren't coming back

lately it feels like I could die from my broken heart
like the tears and the heartache will never stop
and there's nothing you could say or do
to make me forget the way I loved you

if planes could talk
we'd sit here for hours
listening to all the
love stories that
started with the arrival gate
and ended with the departure gate

you had me believing that I meant
more to you than what I actually did
you were always great at making me believe
in lies

there were some nights when I would
cry myself to sleep while you laid
there soundlessly dreaming
I knew deep in my heart
that every kiss goodnight
was leading to a final goodbye

watching you fall in love
with people who aren't me
~things I can't get over

I press play on my favorite sad song
open a bottle of whiskey
and cry a little bit
not loud enough to draw attention
but enough to numb my mind
I down the first shot and
it burns
your memory always burns
I close my eyes and swallow you anyways
~things I do when I start thinking of you

time passes, but the promises remain the same
a little dose of hope mixed in with emptiness
I'm not sure why I put myself in these situations
place my trust in people who've never shown
proof that they've earned it
my friends say that I'm a hopeless romantic
that love will be my undoing one day
I can't help but think they're right
because 26 years later
I'm still clinging to scraps
people offer up whenever they want
something from me
time passes
but I remain the same

I've lost count of how many times
I've said goodbye to you

I know you're out there thinking about them right now. Thinking about the way you met and all your firsts. Thinking about the future you could have had and how it's not promised anymore. Thinking about ways to get them back and waiting for them to return. You wish for them to realize what they lost and to learn to appreciate you for what you gave them. But in case you didn't know, you are also someone who is worth missing. I hope that one day you choose people who choose you too.

you don't need them the way you think you do
you think you need to hear their heartbeat in order
to fall asleep at night
you think you need to feel their arms around you
in order to feel safe and loved
you think you need to see their smile every day
for life to feel meaningful
you think you need them for life to feel full
you think you're nothing without them

but in reality
all you need is you
you were you before they came into your life
you slept soundly at night in your bed
you have an endless capacity
of providing safety and love to yourself
your life had meaning before them
and it still does
you existed before their love
and you will exist after it
give yourself some grace

I wanted to blame you
not just for the way you treated me
but for the way you let me go
quickly and without a second thought
although I don't forgive you for your unkindness
I do recognize that there were days
I chose to break my own heart
I wanted to be the one for you
and I needed you to be the one for me
I put the entirety of my heart into this
and I didn't want to lose
and in the process of loving us
I lost myself
so how can I blame you for my own inability
to recognize when things don't want me?
I don't blame you anymore
on those days
I blame myself

"it's really over, isn't it?"

"ya, I think it is."

how did we get here?
how did it turn from love
to hatred so quickly?
why am I the only one hurting?

this should've never happened
this space between us should've never existed

I want to ask you so many things
but I can't without feeling like
I'll mess something else up

what has become of us?

give me time to heal
to find myself
to bring myself back home

give me time to collect
the pieces you took
the pieces you broke off
bit by bit

I know that I'll find my way
back home again
but please
just give me time

I was searching for a fire in a soul
whose lighter belonged to another
I had convinced myself to fall in love
with a man before I knew
what love was

and my punishment?

confining my soul
in an endless white room
while tears of longing escape
filling my everlasting
life sentence of life in hell
~unrequited love

you were never mine to keep
never mine to love
but I've still got a little bit of you
tucked away in the deepest corners
of my heart

I want a life where I'm welcomed
into your home
not just your bed

How am I supposed to let you go when you won't let me let you go? I don't want half a love, half a person, and I'm not interested in chasing a daydream. So, if you already know what you're looking for, and I'm just not it, don't allow me to continue loving someone who can't reciprocate those feelings. Let me go.

I envy those who've found love

but once I have it
I push it away

sometimes it feels like I have
a heart that's prepared
to destroy anything
and everything
that tries to love it

when you left
I spent countless days picking up
my brokenness from the floor
I spent endless hours gluing
together the delicate pieces

and now that I'm all better

I spend nights upon nights
imagining the exact moment
I get to see your crystal eyes again
the moment I get to see
the regret wash across your face
as you realize that
you lost the very thing you had
spent years praying for

there's a voice in my head that says
I wasn't good enough
that you never loved me at all and
you found better somewhere else
it says you left me for her
because she looked more like the girls
in the magazines
her hair was softer
her eyes were bluer
and she was whole
it says I was too damaged
too hard to love
too complicated to make it work
and that's why giving up on me was easier
I wished I was her
but thank God I'm not
because you tore through her heart
the same way you did mine
I guess it's true
you can't make sense of careless hearts
and your existence will never be enough for them

I wanted to be more than convenient to you
but I guess love with you doesn't work like that

convenience taught me one thing though
and that was when to walk away

How am I supposed to accept that it wasn't me who did everything wrong?

I continued loving you
despite knowing that you
didn't deserve me
I kept supporting you
thinking that you were
going to change
I made excuses for
the relationship thinking
that it was going to be
different this time around
but it wasn't
because I couldn't make
you choose me
or want me
or even remember me
when I was gone

how do you mourn the love that never happened?
the one we never truly experienced?
a love that was full of chaos and tears and what-ifs?
how do we forgive ourselves for the things that
never really became anything?
because those are the worst types of heartaches
the heartaches that are associated with love that
we were never able to hold in our hands

It's a heart-wrenching reality to know that you're holding on to someone who's simultaneously choosing to let you go.

It's a terrifying reality to know the truth, and yet continue to choose to stay in an environment that's choosing to move on without you.

You can be aware that a story is finished and not want to put the book down. You can be aware that this environment isn't what's best for you and not want to leave. You can feel the pain of their betrayal and still want to have the capacity to understand. You can have all the answers laid out in front of you and still choose not to see them.

I promise you,
you are not alone.

You're just trying to honor the love you have for them and the way you feel. Don't hold resentment in your heart for yourself.

Sometimes we choose to make things work, and another person decides that they cannot choose that same reality. And that is okay.

I used to wish that, when you looked me in the eyes, you could see how much I loved you. How much I truly valued your presence in my life. Looking back now, I realize that the way I loved you was only comparable to unrealistic perfection, and dismounting you from the pedestal I had put you on was one of the worst nightmares I've ever had to wake up from. Where I used to see perfection, I now see a person who, over time, and little by little, broke me apart, because you could never admit that you were unhappy.

trying to explain how I feel about you now is difficult
do I love you?
do I hate you?
lately it all feels the same
ask me again tomorrow

when you left
I was finally given the chance
to get to know every single part of me
and what I found
was that you were no longer there

the worst ache comes
when you wake up one day
and there is a heart
that can't be held anymore

when you realize
that you've run out of time
and there is absolutely
nothing you can do

all the *I love you*s
in the world
can never bring
them back

and the piece of your heart
that shattered with their loss
never quite fits the same because
every time you try to put it back
pieces of it fall off

if my heart could hold
on to yours forever
it'd make all the
heartaches before you
worth it

if I'm being honest
I came here to forget you
so, tell me why I see you
staring back at me?
haunting me from these pages?
~writing

you have not truly seen yourself
until you have seen the shattered
pieces of your heart lying bare
in your hands

to the ones who break our hearts:

I hope that you find what you're looking for out there
from the bottom of my heart
I hope you do

I hope you find
the kind of happiness that exists
to make your life feel full
the kind that wraps you up
and hugs you like your parents did
when you were a child every Christmas morning
the kind that I found within you

I hope you truly take the time
that you said you needed
to find what encourages your soul
what dreams you still need to live
and the courage to chase them
I hope you show the world what
you can do with all that
passion and dedication within you
and then I hope it leads you back to me

but if it doesn't

I hope you find the kind of love
that makes you a softer human
the kind that believes in you
and supports you
and makes a home in your heart

the kind that shows you
that you can in fact
love deeply
and give love wholly
and completely

I hope you find something real
and moments that take your breath away
I hope you live and
that life is kind to you
I hope you travel to places that cleanse you
where you can connect with your spirit
and find beauty in simplicity

to the ones who break our hearts:

I truly hope you find yourself out there
I hope you figure out your heart
and your mind
and how to love others properly
I hope you learn to be gentle with yourself
to embrace who you are
and learn to fall in love with the journey
and always remember

when we said we loved you
we did not just mean it
we lived it

it was the feeling in our chest
that was beyond words
the feeling that all our pieces
were coming together
by some unexplainable
magnetic force

it was looking into your eyes
and finding a home

I'm not entirely sure
how to explain the rest to you
so, I'll say the one thing
that might come close

remember how I whispered
"I love you"
into the skin behind your ear
the curve of your spine
the edge of your shoulder blade
it wasn't simply for you to hear
but to feel
the love I had for you

you're at a place right now where
your heart says "keep trying"
when your mind says, "this isn't working"
your thoughts are filled with so much fear
it feels like your soul is spiraling out of control
and letting go is something you struggle with
but let me tell you this
you're not less of a person for walking away
from situations that hurt you
for honoring your boundaries
and moving on from the things that cause you heartache
it makes you brave
it makes you strong
and it shows the love and
respect you have for yourself

Kayla McCullough

I let myself care for a love
that had died a long time ago
I held on for as long as I could
but eventually I found myself saying
"let me go"

you can't keep trading your happiness for theirs
you can't keep fighting for a version of them that doesn't
exist
you can't keep waiting for somebody
who isn't capable of figuring out
that you're also someone who is worth fighting for

the person who can't tell you that they love you
is not somebody who is worthy of your love
who is worthy of breaking your heart

I woke up this morning
and for the first time
in a long time
I didn't want to cry
I didn't check my messages
or want to call you
I didn't see your ghost
as I made my morning coffee
or hear your voice
singing along to the radio
for the first time
in a long time
I didn't think of you at all

you were a slow kind of love
a love that made a point
to come into your life
not to turn your world upside down
but instead to stay
and make a home in your heart
to soothe your soul
a love where you have to listen
to your head
not only your heart
which makes it feel
all that more real
I didn't fall in love with you
because I needed to
I walked into a love
where we both had to
bend over backward to give
each other what we deserved
to make sure we both felt seen
to make sure we both felt heard
I didn't just find the right person
I found the person who became
the right one

I didn't fall in love with you because I needed to
or because I needed someone else to love
God knows I should be loving myself a little bit more
no
you just happened
and I'm happy you happened to me
because I think you might have been everything
I never knew I needed
they say that everything happens for a reason
and I'm so grateful that everything led me to you

I fell in love with you so fast because you made me feel something after being comfortable for so long. You made me feel adventurous, hopeful, and enough. You taught my heart to stop choosing distance over depth and find love in my broken pieces. Thank you for that.

It wasn't the breakup that hurt the most. It was waking up
and checking my phone for the messages that weren't
there anymore. It was going to bed alone and learning
how to deal with the silence once more. It was looking
at our pictures and seeing exactly when you fell out of
love with me—that moment documented for all to see. It
was starting my life over again and not knowing where
to start putting the pieces back together. It wasn't the
breakup that hurt the most; it was the trauma that came
after it.

by the time I was ready to let you go
I'd spent forever waking up beside you
learning the way you liked your coffee
listening to what brought you joy in this world
and consoling you when things didn't go as planned
it was brutal letting all that go
I was suspended in a future
that I thought we both wanted
and now that
that's gone
it feels like I'm suspended in an eternity
of longing and heartache

you were the hardest person I ever had to let go of
the hardest lesson I ever had to learn
and there are days I wonder
what my life would be like if we'd never met
if I never had to force myself to forget
the way your voice sounded
or the way your skin would feel on mine
would my life be easier if we'd never become us?

when you left you never looked back
it was as if you fell out of love with me
before we even knew what love could be between us
and in that moment, I felt like love
would never choose me again

They say that once someone has hurt us, it's harder for us to relax around them and think of them as safe to love. What I think they're also forgetting is that this doesn't stop us from wanting them. It doesn't stop us from having hope that they might come around one day and be the person we knew they could become and love us the way we need to be loved. It doesn't stop us from building up their potential.

if you break up
be the person they never hear from again
the person who goes off
and finds their passion
and lives life without any regrets
and loves fiercely
be the one who lets go
and surrenders to the fact that
the right people exit your life
at the right time
and it's not because you didn't love them
it's because you loved yourself more

there was a time when loving you
had made me hate
how big of a heart I had

not so much for loving and forgiving
those who wrong me

but because of how taxing it was
to try and make you happy

and while I had the daily chore
of proving how much I cared for you
I was still the one
getting hurt
getting taken for granted
and in the end
getting left behind

but I guess there is one good thing
that comes with having a big heart
it had the space for your name to be tattooed on it
and now it no longer has the chore of giving itself out
to those who don't intend to keep it safe

so, in a way, I guess it's free

and the saddest part is
I stayed by your side
long after I knew I wasn't meant
to be there anymore
and healing through how scared I was
to let you go
was one of the worst battles
I think I have ever gone through

I'm over the nausea and the crying
but you're still the first thing I see
as I get up in the morning
and the last
as I close my eyes at night

it wasn't easy picking up
the pieces when you left
figuring out where you ended
and where I began again
without even realizing it
I had lost myself
trying to love you
I had given away everything
trying to be enough for you

when you're fighting for someone
who never existed in the body
you grew to love
to adore
letting go is one of the hardest
things to accept
and when moving on becomes
the only choice
you eventually learn
to let go
because there's more to life
than fighting for someone to change
when they don't want to

I made so many excuses for your behavior
to the people I loved
I had wished away all the lies
all the broken promises
and I had put myself down
to try and build you up
I wished I would have realized
that you were never capable of
becoming the person
I thought you could be sooner
because I wouldn't have wasted so much time
on someone who didn't want my time to begin with

I used to think that the worst thing that could ever happen in life would be to lose something you fought so hard to keep, but it isn't—it's realizing you were holding on to nothing, and the person you loved never existed in the first place.

I broke my own heart trying to make you happy
I broke my own heart trying to fix and love
what I thought was broken within you
and now that you're gone
it's me who must glue it back together
someone won in this
and it wasn't me

I know right now you want to find an answer
an answer to why they moved on from everything so
easily
why it seemed like they slipped away so effortlessly
why letting you go
didn't cost them anything
but I promise you
if you revisit all your memories
every detail
every conversation
will eventually tell its own story
and explain why they're no longer here

if someone's already looking for a way out
you can't hold on to them
no matter how much you love them
they won't stay

it was always my love for you
that made you special
my reasoning and my understanding
that made a home for you to come back to
each time you broke a promise
and I kept putting myself through the pain
of fighting for you because the hope I had
for something more outshone the reality
I wanted to face
I was torn between not wanting to give up
on the person I loved
the person I would do anything
and everything for
and facing the reality that
that person never truly existed in the first place

it was me who made you special
my love for you that made you shine
and now that you're gone
I must take you off that pedestal

you cared about them more
than anyone else in the world
believed that they could change
and you kept loving them even though
they never deserved it
and it was never enough
because they walked away like it was nothing

you were never just another person to me
never just another hand for me to hold
or heart to get to know
learning about the things that made you happy
the things that ignited you
was the best part of my day
you were never wasted time to me
there was never a moment when
you were ever not enough
you were everything to me
so don't tell me letting you go
was easy for me
I gave you everything
every part of me
so, trust me when I say that
one-sided love is not
a love worth keeping

when I wake up each morning
your eyes are the ones I want to meet
your lips are the ones I want to kiss
your body is the one I want to hold
you are the one I choose to fall in love with
every day until my last

loving you was never supposed to be
an emotionally excruciating game
where I sweep red flags under the rug
to keep you from tripping over them

they were the one you pictured
your whole life with
pictured marriage
having kids
growing old together
the future you created
was the one thing you depended on
now it's just another thing
you have to let go of
that isn't real anymore

I thought of you today
it was an unconscious effort
the way you slipped into my mind
it was something I couldn't stop

I thought of the way your hand felt in mine that first time
the way your fingers would swallow my palm
I thought of the way you kissed me under the night sky
the way the light from the moon hit your cheeks
and showed all the lines on your face
all your imperfections that were beautiful to me
I thought of the first time your hands traced my skin
delicately and then fiercely
those hands let me know that I was yours
completely yours

but like all things in life
the bad seem to outweigh the good, and

I thought of our very first fight
I thought of the way you yelled
I thought of the first time I caught you
keeping secrets from me
the things that you never told me
but somehow, I already knew
the ones who made me feel worthless and unloved
the ones who I pushed aside because I loved you

I thought of the disappointment your face showed
the first time you realized
that I may not be what you wanted after all
I thought of the way you started pulling away from me
and the excuses you would say
I thought of the first time you cast me aside
and the way it then became a habit

and then I thought of our last day together
the last day we were two halves of the same whole
the day we talked and cried as we agreed that this was
the end

is there a way I can turn my thoughts off?

I don't know why I kept coming back to you. Why it seemed like a part of my life and a part of my heart would always belong to you. Why I'd always let you back into my life, just because I loved you. You had every opportunity, and you chose to walk away—over and over again. I may still love you, and I may still care for you for the rest of my life, but that doesn't mean you have to be a part of it—so, this is me letting you go.

love with you was a constant cycle of toxic guessing
games, each filled with heartache and lust

sometimes I wish you would have loved me
like I loved you
but then I remember that
love isn't meant to hurt like that
love isn't tears that are drowned out
while you're sitting in your shower
so that nobody hears
love isn't worrying about
the other people they're texting
claiming that they're just friends
love isn't thinking, "I hope he means what he says"
if he actually says what he feels
love isn't any of those things
so, if you would have loved me
like I loved you
I would've never learned
that love was never you to begin with

There are times I wonder what would have happened if we had stayed friends. If our final goodbye never happened, and instead, we removed the labels and muffled our chemistry. Would our story have changed? Would you have eventually fallen in love with me like I had fallen in love with you? Would a friendship in the beginning have changed the heart-aching agony we both felt at the end? I regret not being your friend first.

when you love someone
who only loves you with half their heart
you feel like you don't get enough time
you can feel the ending of your story
even before it's been written
so, you hold on to them
as hard as possible
memorizing moments before they vanish
hoping that they'll feel like home
even after they're gone

sometimes it feels like I failed at loving you
like I never said enough of the right words
to heal your broken heart
and I know that people leave
and hearts break
but when you left
you never looked back
you were okay with losing me
okay with leaving me in your past
and that betrayal left my heart
refusing to let go of any vulnerability
that it had left

I used to think that losing you
was one of the most painful things
that came with trying to love you
but in reality
it was finding out that I had lost myself
in the process of fighting for someone
who was never truly mine from the beginning

there were signs
the conversations grew shorter
the happy days only existed in my memories
and the love was unrequited
yet I still held on
not wanting to let go of something
I had put the entirety of my heart into
yet I blamed you for my inability
to recognize when things should have ended
for that, I'm sorry

letting go wasn't my greatest fear
it was learning that while I was still committed
to loving you
to making this work
you'd already let me go

Kayla McCullough

I don't regret loving you anymore
I don't regret meeting you or
any of the memories we share
what I do regret is knowing
that loving you meant denying
the love I needed to give myself

I regret sacrificing my happiness for yours
and tolerating the ways you hurt me
but most of all
I regret not loving me
while I was loving you

I know that there's a part of you that wants to keep a part of them close to you. You treasured the part of them that was loving, and understanding, and kind. You loved them so much that when they left, they took a piece of your heart, a piece of your life with them. It's hard to carry on without the person you imagined your life with. It's hard to let go of a dream you wanted to become reality, but it's time to let them go. It's time to move on. It's time to start gluing back your heart again, so that one day, hopefully very soon, you can be you again.

I hate to admit it
I really do
but there was a part of me
that wanted to see you again
a part of me that didn't want
the last time I saw you
to have been the last time
I was hoping that there'd be a day
when we'd finally see each other again
and everything would finally feel right
we would finally make sense
that day came
it didn't end the way I had imagined it would
it left me more brokenhearted than before
however, I know that there's still a path for me
life still has incredible things planned for me
and even though you're no longer a part of it
I can't wait for those things to happen
~letting go

You want to stay, even when they don't feel like home anymore, because they are all that you know. They've already seen all your baggage, and you don't want to unpack it for someone else.

one of our pictures showed up
in my memories today
and I let myself look at it
you look different
than what I remember
your hair's longer and
your smile doesn't reach your eyes
I guess it wasn't all in my head
and you fell out of love with me
before I fell out of love with myself

I guess it was better that way
it was easier to convince
my heart to let go of something
that never loved it from the start

maybe you never end up with the person
whom your heart chooses
maybe you learn what you truly want in life
from the people who leave

right person wrong time
that's what we tell ourselves
when they leave
we repeat it over and over again
until even fate could believe it
but somehow, she never does
and instead, she whispers all the reasons
why you were perfect for me then
you taught me how to let go
and how to let others in
taught me how to stop choosing the people
who don't choose me
and to reserve that space for someone kinder
taught me to love myself and all my insecurities
when you couldn't
I realize now that she was right all along
you were the right person at the right time
and entirely the wrong person for
me to spend the rest of my life with

my heart breaks for the girl
who can love a perfect stranger
in a heartbeat
but endlessly struggles
to love herself

lately I've been wanting to be everyone
and everything else but me

I struggle with loving myself and I don't know why. Finding self-love, accepting your flaws, respecting who you are, and aiming to be the best version of yourself, is all anyone talks about. Yet, I continually fail at seeing who that person is.

Does my highest self wake up in the morning without fuss? Does she hustle and get a workout in before her morning coffee? Is her day filled with empathy for others and love for herself? Is she kind and soft and sweet? Because when I close my eyes and I picture what the greatest me is, despite the turmoil and heartache she's gone through, that's her; however, my life doesn't look like that. So which part of me is worthy?

We preach self-love and self-worth, yet no one knows exactly what that looks like. I'm not less of the greatest version of me because I'm not sure which part of my life led me to not want to look in the mirror. I'm not less of the greatest version of me because I'm not sure which part of my life led me to pick apart my insecurities. I'm not less of a person because there are parts of myself that I'd rather keep hidden.

So, what is it? What makes you worthy?

Maybe I'm just overthinking, but I believe that we're all doing the best we can, and we must grant ourselves room to grow. Too often we get caught up in trying to control every aspect of our life, from how our day looks, all the way down to who we are as a person. But if we acknowledge those things and remind ourselves that we have an infinite amount of room to grow, I believe we open space in our hearts to start accepting who we are as we show up and we begin to fall in love with our journey.

you bottle up your emotions and
hold back your thoughts
because you fear upsetting them
you offer up apologies
and promises
even after they've hurt you

you break your own heart
trusting theirs once more

you fall in love with potential
because you want to see the good in people

you give and give your love
without ever receiving theirs in return

but the day has come
and you've had enough

Kayla McCullough

you're tired of never being enough

you're learning to let go of
broken promises and
picking yourself up to glue
your heart back together

you realize that your existence and love
may never be enough for them

but you are enough for you
and that is all that matters
~overlover

You feel like you lost yourself a long time ago and you've just been pretending to be okay. That, if you close your eyes long enough, all the broken pieces will disappear. That, if you smile hard enough, you'll be happy. But you've always been important. You've always been more than what has hurt you. More than your past mistakes and traumas. And you will always be enough.

sometimes the things that people
don't want to share with the world
the things they think are ugly
or scary
are often the reasons why
we love them so much

I know you feel broken
but you are not broken

I know you feel alone
but you are not alone

I know you feel lost
but you are not lost

there must be something wrong with me
because I'm beginning to believe
that most people
don't mean what they say

loving someone who doesn't love you back
feels a lot like loving denial
you keep reading the story
even after it's over
because if you don't
all you're left with is the truth
and that leaves you not knowing
how to think about them
without feeling like you're losing them
all over again

it was complicated
that's what we tell ourselves
when things don't go
the way we imagined them
it was everything I wanted
you were everything I needed
and maybe that's why it seemed
nearly impossible to let it all go
I wish someone would have
told me sooner that sometimes staying
and hoping for things to change
hurts you more than
them coming clean and
telling you the truth to your face
and maybe even then
I wouldn't want to believe it
so, I'll sit here
and keep believing
that it was complicated

you've already broken
all your boundaries
to continue loving them
and to continue working on things
but have you noticed
that the effort you're putting in
is breaking you more
than helping you?

there came a point when
fighting for your love
became all that I knew
I was convinced that
I needed your love to feel whole
when in reality
it was your love ripping
my heart apart
and at some point
it just got too hard to keep fighting
the damage you caused
and the lies you told
it was too much
especially when I lost sight
of what I was fighting for

I think I'm doing something wrong with my life
everywhere I look, people my age are
getting married
having babies
buying homes
excelling at their career
or accomplishing it all
all at once
there must be something I'm doing wrong
because it seems like I'm not doing anything right
every day, I fail at something
and the irony is
that's the one thing I'm good at
failing

while others sleep at night
my mind races
I think
did I make the right choice?
why did I do that?
why did I say those things?
will they stop loving me one day?
did they ever love me?
when will I be happy?

they must think
I'm doing something wrong with my life
because if I'm thinking those things
then they must be thinking them too
~life of an overthinker

it's true, I'm not for everyone
but not everyone is for me
and that's a hard thing to accept

I don't know if love will ever find me
but I know that I'm worthy of it
and that's all that matters

Kayla McCullough

I think it's sad
that we as a society
have this misconception that if
you look a certain way
or if your life reflects a certain beauty
people won't tear through you
we accept that the grass is greener somewhere else
and run to abandon our home for it
but none of that's true
there's no standard for beauty
and you can't make sense of
someone else's perception of it
just like you can't make sense
of someone's ability
to destroy you

sometimes I wonder
what my life would look like
if I had stayed

if I didn't get the urge
to spread my wings
and fly away

would I be as happy as I am
in this moment with you?

would I feel as free or *me*
in a town without you?

sometimes I get the urge
to go back home
to visit family
or to grow alone

what happens if I decide to stay?
does everything I've worked toward
everything I care about
go away?

I'm not sure if that's a risk
I'm willing to take

the sadness that has coursed through my life
can be found in the spaces between
the fragments that make up my heart

I have always believed in something more
a life filled with beauty
a love filled with magic

I believe in adventures at sunrise
and coffee at midnight

I believe in strangers becoming family
and family that become strangers

I believe that the moon brings stories
and the sun holds promises and
that every star has a wish to tell

I believe that cardinals are our angels
and butterflies are our guides and
that every animal can talk

I believe in love
in a love that never lets us go

I believe in loving so deeply that it breaks us
in a love that shatters our very soul

I believe that hearts can heal
and that when it's all said and done
there is even more love and softness
in them than before

I believed in love when my heart broke
I believed in love when it felt like
I couldn't love anymore

I believe in there being more

I believe in fate
and that coincidences are more
than coincidences

I believe that we are made up of stardust
that we are the same as the space above us

I believe that when we ask for answers
we are met with them tenfold

I believe in the unknown
I believe in the things that we can't explain
the very things that weave our lives together
and make them alive

I believe in the magic of our life

when you are ready
life will hand you everything
and say, "this is what you deserve.
treat it with all the kindness and love
that's in your soul."

when you have a broken heart
you learn to live with the wounds
not fully recovering
not fully forgiving
you learn to live with the memories
of them engraved throughout your body

when you have a broken heart
you forget that somewhere in your chest
the broken pieces are intertwining themselves together
fusing lost love with future hope
you barely even recognize it, but
you're being put back together
every day

Your healing won't happen overnight, because moving on is never easy. No matter how simple others like to make you believe that it is, it's not.

Healing is a process that takes its time. It's a journey that doesn't have a clear destination because it's a journey that never stops. You are constantly healing, and whether you know it or not, you've been doing it your whole life.

When you were 15, you cried over your first love. When you were 19, you let go of friendships that you thought were going to be in your life forever. When you were 22, you grieved over losses and experiences you wanted to forget. In every situation that you didn't know how to move on from, somehow, you did. What if, instead of believing that your healing is one destination, you began to recognize that it's life's way of moving you forward?

Healing isn't about reaching one point and then forgetting how you got there. It's not about pushing away the pain but allowing the pain, and the heartbreak, and the losses, to become part of who you are. Healing doesn't happen overnight; it's constantly happening.

Every tear, every laugh, and every experience is moving you in another direction, so that you can become who you were always meant to be.

sometimes I think it would have been easier
if you'd given me a reason to hate you
a reason to forget your memory
a reason to forget the way your voice sounded
a reason to forget everything that replays in my mind
every time I go to sleep at night

but moving on doesn't mean forgetting
it just means learning how to live again
learning how to live without you

I believe that there's a reason why your heart connects to certain people more than others. Why a specific person will leave a lasting footprint on your life. You can call it fate or a coincidence, but I believe that there's something out there bringing us closer to those who will teach us important lessons about life and ourselves. The sad truth is that most of the people who touch our hearts are temporary. They're not meant to stay forever. They're only here to show us a different way and then to set us free.

I was so sure that our story
was written in the stars
that your love was true
and we were meant to be
but look at us now
I'm sifting through old texts
trying to piece together
where it all went wrong
and you're busy kissing
other hearts
trying to find another story
that belongs

when you left, I woke up to you everywhere
I saw you lying next to me in bed
smelled remnants of your shampoo on the pillowcase
felt your hand brush against mine
I woke up to you everywhere and yet
you were nowhere to be found
so, I brushed you out of my hair
washed you out of my sheets
and tucked you away as I made my bed
I let life fade the memory of you

"What if I told you I've loved you all this time," he says, hesitating and reaching for my hand. I smile. I wipe the tears away. I accept his embrace and fall into his warmth. I step back and look up at the night sky, stars spanning as far as the eye can see. I try not to think about how much I've been wanting to hear his voice and those exact words—about how much those words hurt. How they sound more like an insult than a loving gesture, even when I've been waiting for this moment for years.

I love you. Those were the words that my heart wanted to hear while I was flying across the country to see you. The tears were rolling down my face, and I wished for them to stop. I wished that no one could see my silent cries. I wished I could be stronger, less attached, care less.

I love you. Those were the words that I wanted to hear after our fight about you staying at another girl's house. "She's just a friend," you said.

I didn't know friends acted like that.

I love you. Those were the words that I thought I was going to hear back after pouring my heart out to you that night in your kitchen. The same night I was trying to decide what the rest of my life was going to look like. If after all this time and choosing you over everything else even mattered to you.

It didn't.

What if I told you I've loved you all this time was indeed an insult to how much I loved you and how much I fought for you.

What if I told you I've loved you all this time felt more like betrayal to who you are than love would ever feel to me.

"And what if I told you, after all this time, that your love no longer has a home in my heart," I say. I wipe the tears away and open my eyes.

He's gone and I'm staring through the blackness of my bedroom and up at the ceiling.

~closure

I have a bad habit of imagining endings
I close my eyes and cling to happiness
I think it's because I grew up watching love stories
and wishing on stars
but with how many scars line my heart
you'd think by now I'd know that
not every story has a happy ending
and not every princess finds true love
so today I asked my heart to explain why
it finds comfort in naivety
and she said, "I find comfort in the color red."
~red flags

I'm beginning to think that the distance
that separated our hearts
was the thing that made me
love you harder

I know now that this isn't how love works
you don't get to pick and choose which parts
of me you want to love
you don't get to hide me away
offering me visiting hours
when it suits you

love isn't meant to hurt you
it isn't meant to make you feel
small or like you're never enough

you're worth being committed to
you deserve to be seen and understood

no, you won't find a love that's perfect
but you will find a love that reminds you
of how perfect you are for them
you deserve to be held and cared for
the same way you hold and care for others
never forget that

There are times when I think I've healed from you, and then, out of nowhere, it hits me again. The memories of us come flooding back like they were never supposed to leave in the first place, and I'm left reminiscing on what could have been. During those moments, I swear I can almost touch you—and it feels like I never healed at all. I'm stuck in a cycle of *moving on today* and *falling apart tomorrow*. But I guess that's the thing with healing— because even on the days when it doesn't feel like I'm moving on, I know that if I look back and remember all the nights I laid awake crying, those memories will outweigh the good ones. I never want to feel like that again, and that is what I call growth.

I have a heart that's used to
absorbing love from
the wrong people
it overlooks flaws
and gets taken advantage of
it empathizes with strangers
and trusts too quickly
it hurts itself by not letting go
it breaks from the chances it
gives to those who fail to show up
and it bleeds from the weight of
placing love on a pedestal
and when you left it alone
dying in the cold
it was a wonder it was able
to stand up again
and find forgiveness

it's true
I have a heart that's naive
it loves a little too much
but it's strong
and if it can withstand
a love from the wrong place
it was made to survive anything

I used to think that people
who leave people
were never in love
but after loving you
I know that's not true
sometimes people leave people
not because they're not in love
but because the love they existed in
was never love at all

I mailed your hoodie back to you today
even though it might seem insignificant
the last time we spoke
you told me to keep it
like I needed a reminder
that you were someone who kept me warm
someone I ran to for comfort
and if that's the case
you didn't know me at all and
what they say is true
I'm better off without you
because I don't need a possession
to remind me of you
I see you in every summer day
I see you in the morning as I make my coffee and
at night as I close my eyes
I see you in every song I hear
and every line I write
I don't need a reminder
that you were my everything in life
I need to learn to exist in a world
where you're no longer a part of it

I mailed your hoodie back to you today
it's insignificant
not heroic at all
and to some
it might even be melodramatic
but to me
it was healing

At some point, I stopped sending you the love letters I wrote, and I started releasing them to the wind, thinking maybe they'd reach you faster. Years later, I think someone else opened them, because the wind brought a promise home from a stranger, and my heart no longer is a home for yours.

if they stop choosing you one day
I hope you remember that
it doesn't mean you're unlovable
or that you're not enough
I hope you don't blame yourself
or ever think that
it's a direct representation
of who you are
because it's not
sometimes people leave our lives
not because of what we did
or who we are
but because their part
in our story is finished
and closed chapters never lead
to happily ever afters

I never wanted to choose between
the people I loved and
who I needed to love more

what I've learned is that
saying goodbye to the people
you love most
is a form of self-love
a form of peace
because if they were truly
meant for you
you wouldn't have lost yourself
in the process of trying to love them

you deserve everything in this world
and if that's a world without them in it
that's okay

Your heartbreak is supposed to hurt, because the love you felt for them was real for you. Whether or not it was real for them doesn't matter, because what you felt was genuine. The love you gave them was real. Just because you ended up loving the wrong person doesn't mean there's anything wrong with you. It doesn't mean there's anything wrong with how you love others. It just means that it wasn't supposed to be, and that's okay. Where you are right now is temporary. What you're feeling right now is only for a season. So, honor your heartbreak, accept that they were here for a reason, and let it go.

you may not want
to let them go right now
you may never want
to let them go
but continuing to chase them
will never be worth the heartache
it will never be worth the self-doubt
or uncertainty
feeling your heart break
into a million pieces
each time they choose
someone or something else
is no way to live
it's no way to love

so, it's time to let them go
it's time to move on
it's time to get to know you again
the real you
the you without them

I knew that I was healing
when your inconsistent behavior
no longer surprised me
when I was no longer waiting
for you to show up
to come around
to change
or tell me what I wanted to hear
when I stopped trying so hard
for you to do so little for me
I'm not interested
in your approval anymore
nor do I need it
I'm not interested in waiting
for your half-truths
to become full-ass lies
nor do I want them
I now know that it's better
to let things and people go
and to be on my own
than to stay and fight a losing battle

I threw my journals out today
the ones that were littered with your presence
they were the last physical tie
I had to you in this world
I kept them as a reminder of when I started
romanticizing our time together again
it worked, and
somehow after years of silence from you
I'm finally okay enough to rid myself of them
~growth

there's a part of you that will always know
when you should let go
of anything in life
it's like the essence of who you are knows
that your heart will never find peace
if it's confined to loving something
that doesn't love it
never mistake those gut feelings
because once you move on from something
that causes your heart to be so heavy
you'll see that it was always standing in your way

you never thought you'd experience it
a heartbreak so profound that it changes your life
one minute they're there
saying all the perfect things
convincing you of their love
and the next they're gone
months have gone by
and your heart's still on the bathroom floor
the shattered pieces growing with every tear
you think you're broken
and you'd do anything to stay invisible
because you can't bear the guilt
of them seeing you cry
and you don't think they'd understand
but I see you
even on the days when you can't see yourself
I see you, and trust me
the world is better with you in it
let this heartbreak change your life for the better

don't change yourself to make them love you more
in the end, the only person you'll lose is yourself

Kayla McCullough

the one thing this heartache
has taught me
is that you are going to grieve
as deeply as you loved

but don't let that stop
you from choosing
to love deeply
because
grief is
the final act of love

maybe losing them
is the turning point
in your life

it's okay to let the tears
wash you clean

heartbreak has taught me many things
but the most important one is that
healing does not mean
becoming the best version of yourself
you are always worthy
of everything in life
healing means accepting
that there's a worst version of you
that needs to be loved

the hardest part about letting them go
is learning how to unlove them
so that the hope of them returning
diminishes little by little
because you've already wasted so much
of your time overthinking
and overanalyzing and blaming
yourself for them leaving
and there is so much more to life
than wishing for them to come back

you're not meant to hold on to something
that doesn't want to stay

you were the only person
in the whole world
who understood me
who would glue me back together
when life would break my heart
the one person who would
tell me the truth
no matter how much it hurt
you'd tell me he was no good for me
that he never cared how he hurt me before
and that this time is no different
I'd never listen
I'd always run back into his arms
and then back into yours when
he proved that you were right
I don't know why
life took you away from me
because when I needed someone the most
you weren't there
no one was there
they say friendships come and go
but somehow, I thought
you'd always be around
life has a way of taking things
and then providing you with others
you never knew you needed
it took losing you
to learn how to be there for me

it's hard for you to see it now
but the ache you feel
deep within your heart
is here to guide you
to a love that
won't tear you apart

I wish they had the strength to fight for you
to understand that you were always enough
and that they never needed to mold you or
to fold you away into the corners of their heart
that you were made to be shown off
and to love unconditionally
until the end of time
I wish they had the nerve to show you
every inch of their mind
good and bad
that they never needed to be afraid of being
themselves around you
I wish they were brave enough to show you their love
to wrap it around you
and to let it grow until
their roots intertwined with yours
I wish they were your home
but sometimes coins remain lost in fountains
and stars don't shine bright enough
and that's not because our wishes mean nothing
it's because nothing is sometimes better than
what we think is our everything

missing you comes in waves
it's no longer consuming
just little moments

Have you ever asked yourself why they haven't come back into your life yet? It's been ages after the breakup, and you're just sitting and wondering when they're going to realize what they lost. You pray and ask God if they could just reach out one more time, and those prayers always come unanswered. So, you make excuses and continue to wait for this person, who doesn't even deserve you, to come crawling back. But the thing is, the silence is your answer. Every morning when you wake up with no text or call from them, that's God's way of telling you that you deserve more and that this person isn't worthy of your love and attention. And once you realize that you deserve someone who's going to be there and value you and the attention and the love you give them, that's when life will give you all that you're asking for.

You're still reminiscing on the memories you share with them. You keep thinking about all your firsts—your first kiss, the way they looked at you and smiled every morning when you woke up, the good-morning texts, and the adventures you took. You can't help it, but digging up these memories simultaneously comes with the hope that fate will bring them back to you one day.

You wait, and wait, and wait, but to no avail; they don't come.

If this is you, I want you to remember a few things:

The sad part about love and relationships is that sometimes we develop connections with people who don't appreciate us the way we appreciate them. Who don't love us the same way or see the relationship the way we see it.

But these people, the people who we claim are our soulmates, the people we would do anything and everything for, teach us that sometimes to love unconditionally means to let go. Not everyone is meant to stay in our lives forever—there are some people who are only meant to be fleeting moments—and when these people leave, we will carry a piece of them in our hearts forever. That's just how loving someone works; however, if they loved you with the same force that you loved them, nothing would keep them from you. Sometimes we must lose something and let it break us to remember just how strong we are.

the thing that they don't tell you
about healing is that
when I look in the mirror and
see my reflection
I also see parts of you
forged within it

sometimes we have to move on
from them and the relationship
not because we don't care anymore
but because they don't care anymore

no matter how much you want them
you can't fight for them to love you
so, when they leave and don't say why
you can find closure in knowing that
the right kind of love
will never leave you
questioning your worth
questioning if you were enough
will never leave you
crying over someone who
was okay with losing you
who was okay with letting you go

at some point, I knew that I had to let you go
not because I stopped loving you
but because my heart couldn't hold on to
any more of the hope I was trying to feed it

hope that one day you'd come back
and save me from this heartache

I may never know why
you did what you did

but I can't keep waiting
for the day that you will show me
everything your heart had said it would

it's better to be alone
than to be with people
who make you feel lonely

find a love that makes
the drive to see them
and the distance
between you two
worth it

everything has a breaking point
and when it comes to your broken heart
there's only so many times
you can piece it back together
before you realize you don't want to
go through that pain again
it's okay to love them
and not want to take them back

how much love
do you have to give away
before you realize
that you are deserving
of some too?

it won't hurt as much as it used to
and it's not because your love for them
will mean less as the days pass
it's because as the days come
each morning brings a promise
and each night it honors it
every time you open your eyes
and they're not there
time brings your heart a path
for it to come home

the realization will be quiet
it'll creep up on you
when you least expect it
you'll start to question
why you stay
and doubt if their love
was ever true
please don't ignore this plea
because this is you
telling you
that their love was
never bathed in honesty

you deserve more

You are not responsible for fixing someone. It is not your job to heal them and make them reveal hidden parts of themselves. No matter how much you want to show them the good parts about love and rewrite their stories, if someone doesn't want to open their heart to you and let you in, that's okay. It doesn't mean you failed at loving them.

don't wish for things to have been different
don't try to figure out ways to make them stay
in your life a little longer
don't romanticize the time that you had with them

just learn to accept that some people
come and go from your life
and the people who go
leave for a reason

you deserve to make meaningful connections
with people who make an effort to be in your life

sometimes loving them means
loving yourself more
it's okay to let go

trust me
you will never lose
what is meant for you
if it's right
it will come back

Sometimes the love that you want isn't the love you deserve. There isn't going to be perfection. The kind of person who says or does the right thing all the time doesn't exist; however, real love does. You deserve real, passionate, dedicated, and consistent love. Never settle for anything less than that.

I didn't let you go
because it was easy
or because I wasn't sure of you
or because I hated you
and it would make me happy
it was quite the opposite
I let you go
because I don't deserve
to be some convenient relationship
you want to put effort into at midnight
I let you go
because I don't deserve
to hold on to something
that doesn't want to stay
I chose to let you go
because I don't deserve a love
I have to force, and
you don't deserve to have to feel
something you can't
I tried to be enough for you
I tried to make you stay
I tried to love your heart back together
but I can't fix
what was never whole to begin with

Kayla McCullough

it's not about how or why you left my life
it's not about the memories
or how you used to make me happy
it's about how I thought I needed you
in my life to be loved
it's about how I was so wrapped up
in trying to be loved by you
that I forgot I survived once without you
I don't need you in order to be happy
I can let you go
and find happiness on my own

you say that your heart is broken
and that love doesn't remember you
but you forget
that in some storylines
you are unforgettable
your lips are still the ones they wish to kiss
your hands are still the ones they wish to hold
your hair reminds them of summer days
and your eyes are the ones they see
when they say goodnight
some souls can't let you go

you're not forgettable
so never believe
that someone can come
into your life
and then leave it without
a second thought
you are worth remembering

when they come back
whispering sweet nothings
and begging for your love again
tell them that your heart isn't
a convenient toy to mess with
when they're lonely at 2 am
tell them it's still full
from the lies they fed it
and it's still bleeding from
the empty promises
that sliced through it
when they come back
wanting what they
threw out like garbage
tell them how hard you cry
remembering how they left

I'm not good at goodbyes
but what I've learned is that there
almost always comes a time to move on
a time for a new beginning
in a new home
surrounded by strangers that become friends
it's never easy finding the reason
to why things had to end
searching for closure where there isn't any
and like I said
I'm not good at goodbyes
but if we're being honest
I think I've always loved them
because starting over has always been my redemption
it's something that makes me believe
in the beauty of hope
of the future
of letting go

Sometimes we give people too much credit for the good things they do in our life and too many excuses for the bad things, therefore making these relationships harder to let go of. It's not because they're irreplaceable; it's because, deep down, you know that you've invested way more than what you should have, you've trusted a little too quickly, and you're not ready to face those consequences. If someone is pushing you away, you must let them go, because it's not your job solely to keep everything from falling apart.

Kayla McCullough

If you ever decide to let them go, just know that was one of the bravest things you could've ever done for yourself. Because you can't keep rationalizing their behavior just to keep them in your life a little bit longer—to keep loving them a little bit longer. You're the kind of person who gives endless chances to people and accepts them for who they are, not what they've done. So, if you ever let them go, I hope they know that it took everything in you to do so.

I believe that everything happens for a reason. People leave and love fades so that you can learn to let go. Stories end before you're ready so that you learn to appreciate them while they're being told. Bad things happen to good people so that greater things can fall into their lives. Sometimes goodbyes aren't goodbyes at all. Sometimes they're just bridges to new beginnings. Everything you lose at some point will become something you are grateful for.

saying goodbye isn't always a bad thing
just remember that right now
your heart isn't where theirs belongs
and it's not because you did something wrong
it's because life has other plans in store for you
other hearts for you to meet
your story is just beginning
let the chapters unfold

remind yourself to trace
the fragmented lines
covering your heart
you will remember all
you have sacrificed
all that you
have fought for
you will remember all
you have believed in

if you ever want to heal
from the trauma you have endured
sometimes the best thing
you can do
is remove yourself
from the ones who will cause
the most harm

it's okay to let go
of the things you don't want to let go of
it's okay to move on
from the things you love most in this world
because whatever you're searching for
might just be at the end of that road

I'm not saying that I'm going to be happier without you, just that I'm done begging for you to stay. I'm done waiting for you to decide if you want me, and I'm learning to let go and move on with my life. Because if somebody isn't sure if they want to be with you, you have to promise yourself that you're not going to wait around for them to stay. Sometimes endings aren't even bad. Sometimes endings aren't even endings, they're just bridges to new beginnings.

It is difficult to let go—to move on. It will break you in ways you never thought possible. It will make you bleed in ways you never expected and show you things you'd rather forget. It's easy to succumb to the pain and move through life like it never happened. Remind yourself that, in order for you to be repaired, a part of you must shatter.

heal
not to get them back
but to let go
and find yourself

Your healing won't always look like packing up their stuff and mailing it back to them. It won't always be a straight line, going from point A to point B. There isn't a box next to a checklist that you get to check off once you accomplish something. Healing is a roller coaster. It happens in ways we don't always understand or expect. Some days, you feel like you're on top of this world and the past is behind you, while others feel like there's no future ahead—like nothing in the world will be able to fix what's broken inside you.

Healing happens while you break down in the shower, letting the tears flow to cleanse your soul. It happens when you wake up in the middle of the night all alone, and you're reminded that you have to start and finish each day without them. Healing happens on days when you feel everything, all at once, and on days when you can't feel anything at all. And on those days, your body feels heavy, your mind is groggy, and your heart feels like it's been ripped from your chest. Healing is painful, and you won't always have a visible scar to show that you made it through, but your heart will wear this experience like there are scars, and whenever you look at them, you'll be reminded just how far you've made it.

Most of the time we don't ever feel like we are healing, but we are, little by little, every day.

They may not have loved you the way you loved them, and it may seem like they left you with nothing, but that's not true. You see, they gave you something—they left you with the ability to start choosing yourself. They taught you what love isn't, so that one day you'll know what love is. They taught you what's truly worth fighting for—a love that doesn't require you to sacrifice the best pieces of who you are. Sometimes people come into our lives and they love us in halves. They hollow us out, keep us hanging on by a thread, and make us question if we were ever enough from the beginning. This isn't real love; this isn't honest love. But what you must realize is that it's still a love worth remembering—for the simple fact that it taught you how to walk away from the people who don't know how to love you, and to stand up for who you are and the way you exist in this world.

not everything in life
is attached to your worthiness
or something you did wrong

I promise you
that there is someone
out there who loves you

you can't choose who you fall for
but can choose who you walk away from
and as much as it breaks your heart
I hope you choose you
I hope you choose to let it go
because prioritizing your peace
is never something to feel
ashamed about

love isn't about losing yourself in someone
it's not about being so overwhelmed by them
that parts of you disappear
love is a choice
a decision
an action
a movement
it's not something you must have to complete you
it's discovering that your life was full before
and falling for this person
somehow
makes you feel even more complete

when you left
it was my family
and my friends
that healed a heart
they never broke
I will cherish them
beyond anything
in this world

when you've been hurt so much in the past
I think that there's a part of you that
will always assume that everyone
is going to hurt you
and if you are one of those people
I hope you always see yourself as
someone worthy of love
as someone worthy to be valued
by someone else
I hope you never wait for the things
that didn't choose you first
because you don't ever deserve to feel
like you're becoming less and less important
to the people who mean the most to you

all I ever wanted was closure from you
to know the truth to why you left and
how you could leave so easily
it's only now that I recognize
closure comes from just letting things be
and knowing that your worth doesn't come from
whether someone stays or leaves your life

your scars are proof
of how graciously
and beautifully
you have healed

instead of ruminating over the fact
that the relationship is over
love the fact that it happened

every time I have loved
and my heart has broken
and I didn't think that
I would ever be whole again
pieces of me came back
little by little
over time

my heart came back
a little more whole
a little more complete and
a little more firm in knowing who I am

every time I have broken
and I have let love go
love has held my hand on the way out
she's pointed to the stars
and has wished for me to understand
that just because certain love does not last
it does not mean that it was not a love
worth experiencing

the lines on your heart
are the places where
the light will enter

you are built with every broken piece
you chose to mend back together

sometimes doing what's best for them
is figuring out what's best for you

they didn't take the best of you
and the parts that they did take
let them keep
because life has a way of replacing
things that left with something that
you never knew you needed

you are worthy enough of someone's time
and you are deserving enough to be their treasure
you are more valuable than someone's broken promises
and you are more cherished than their half-truths
don't ever go to bed wanting something
from someone who won't give it to you

three things your heart needs to accept

number one,
how they treat you is how they feel about you

number two,
no response is a response

number three,
there's a huge difference between
someone being the right person for you
and making someone become the right person for you
a love you must force
will never be a love that is right

never go through life searching
for answers in others
your worth comes from within

We place too much emphasis on finding our soulmate.
We believe that if we find someone who is worthy of our
love, somehow, we are complete. But I disagree. While
finding someone to spend our life with does fill up parts
of our soul, it's not something you should dedicate your
life to searching for. You can search this entire world,
this universe, or galaxies in between, for someone more
deserving of your love than yourself, but you'll never find
them. Because you, yourself, deserve your love more
than anyone else.

I think there was a part of you that knew all along how the relationship was going to end.

"I don't want to end up hurting you," you said.

Even though you claimed that you never wanted to hurt me, somehow in the end, I was the one who ended up hurting for the both of us.

And I learned that, *I don't want to end up hurting you,* translated to, *it's not my feelings that scare me, it's yours.*

I thought I was going to be heartbroken forever
I thought a part of myself would never move on
never heal completely
and after a love like that
maybe you're not meant to
maybe you're meant to stay
a little bit broken
a little incomplete

so, imagine my relief
when a day passed and
your name hurt a little less

you didn't seem so extraordinary anymore
and letting you go didn't seem
as impossible as it once did

sometimes love looks like fights at 3 am
and silence during car rides
other times it looks like holding hands
while you're walking
and dance parties in the kitchen

find someone who fights to fix things
and makes life feel full

it's time for you to be happy again
to fill your heart with what makes you feel alive
because life waits for nobody
and you're not responsible for other people's happiness
so, make life happen for you again
prioritize your happiness
and be who you were always meant to be
that is all you need to do in this world

if I am to be loved, let it grow with me
if I am to feel sad, let it move within me
if I am to fight, let it fight for me too

if I am to move on, let me let it go

I knew I was healing
when the person I missed the most
wasn't you
it was me

I knew I was healing
when the feeling of being enough
for myself
and feeling confident in my own skin
and feeling at home in my own soul
outweighed the love I wanted to give to you

I'm not interested in molding myself
into your life anymore

the way forward might be new and unfamiliar
and sometimes lonely

but the person I am now is a whole lot stronger
than the person I was when I was with you

I no longer accept inconsistencies
or broken promises
if someone is walking out of my life
I let them go
because it's easier to adjust my life to their absence
than to adjust my boundaries to their disrespect
I'm not looking for some grand love story
I'm looking for someone who wants
to walk life's journey with me
so, I'm letting you walk away
because you were never the one
and that's okay

you can want to help someone
and still set boundaries with them

you can validate their feelings
and still honor your space

boundaries and empathy
can coexist

the breakup was never
a reflection of your love
or your worth

they could only love you
to the extent of which they loved themselves
they could only understand your heart
with the same capacity as how they understand theirs
they could only show up for you
in the same way they show up for themselves

it was never about you
or the way you loved them
it was always a reflection
of their truest qualities

the things that you don't want to talk about
are the very things that make you
strong
and beautiful
and unique
they are what make you
you
and that's a very special thing

I will give you my heart
on one condition
you must promise
to be gentle with it
you must promise
to treat it with all the love
that you are capable of
it has endured too many battles
and demons
weathered through too many
harsh winters and scorching summers
I will give you my heart
but you must be kind
you must be gentle

I'm not going to fight for you to love me
I've spent too long counting all the reasons why
other people should be loved and
not long enough on why I'm worth loving too

you've spent far too long overthinking and overanalyzing
all the things they said to hurt you
you've been destroying your heart
and your mind
and your soul
seeking the answer to why it had to happen
but to be clear
you did nothing wrong
and you owe it to yourself
to move on from them
you owe it to yourself
to try and heal what they broke

never again will you beg others
to fight for a love
that they don't want

never again will you compromise
your mental wellbeing
to solely sustain a relationship

never again will you give pieces
of your heart away to those
who do not intend to keep them safe

never again will you grasp at
scraps of affection

never again

the only person
you have to be enough for
is you

the only person
you have to make happy
is you

the only love from someone
who matters the most
is from you

their definition of you
doesn't matter
the reason they left your life
doesn't matter

the way you treat yourself
is what matters the most
in this world

I first learned how to ride a horse in the yard behind the house that raised me. Excitement swept across my body as I flung myself on top of her back. I could almost hear my heart beating, and I could taste the happiness that was flowing through my veins. I felt alive.

For the first few weeks, I wasn't allowed to ride alone. If I wanted to spend time with the horses, that time was only to be spent brushing them. But when I was allowed to ride, my dad would lead me around the yard, never taking his hands off the reins and never letting her go faster than a trot. That initial excitement turned into anger. I wanted the freedom to ride alone. I wanted to go faster and be able to feel the wind in my hair. Thinking of falling and colliding with the dirt could have kept me from moving too fast, but I wanted to feel alive again. I wanted to be that girl in the books. The one whose life was perfect because she could do anything. The one who never feared falling, simply because it never happened. So, one night, I snuck out of the house and saddled her up. I rode around the yard and was quickly reminded how alive I was. She spooked from an animal crossing the ditch and reared, and I fell—hard. My head hit the gravel we were trotting over, and it bled.

After that, I feared riding. I didn't want to fall and feel that pain again. That time, it only took a few days for my head to heal, but what if the next time was worse? I let the fear of not getting hurt outshine the beauty riding could bring to my life.

And while my dad was pretty upset that I crossed a boundary, all he said was, "If you fall, you have to get back on." So, out we went and together we rode around the barn.

I learned that sometimes it's best to take things slow and let a bond grow instead of forcing something too fast. I learned that when we start something new, failure is almost always a guarantee, and the longer you sit there feeling sorry for yourself, the more you deprive yourself of the life you were meant to live. I learned that, with every situation you encounter, you will learn and grow from the experience, and if you're met with failure, you will learn to avoid the situation that led to the crash in the first place.

you start to heal the day you separate
who they are and the hurt they caused you
from who you are and the pain you endured

I never told you this
but I'm happy
we didn't work out
since you've been gone
life's been good to me
it's taught me that
I deserve to be loved
without condition
and that love with you
was conditional

love has a learning curve
it takes time to get it right
we will fail
and there will be mistakes
but with practice and patience
we learn how to properly love others
don't feel disheartened
because you got it wrong
feel encouraged and persist
to get it right

I wear my heart on my sleeve
and I still confuse people

I have a happy personality
with sad eyes

I'm outgoing
but still prefer to be alone

there are days when I'm confident
and others when I hide away

I love hard
and yet I've been told that
I'm hard to love

I overshare
and then I overthink

there are days when I think I'm healed
and then the next, I'm hurting again

I'm still trying to find my equilibrium, and that's okay

it was while I was broken
that I truly felt beautiful
it's where my soul found peace

I smile because I know there's more to life
than pining over something that's gone

you haven't heard the poems yet
or maybe you have
maybe you've been checking in on me, and
you're reading this right now
seeing if some part of you lived on
while you've been gone
you always told me you would
told me that love wasn't meant for your heart
but would find a home in countless others
you always had a passion for your games
liked to dig around in other people's love and
made them dig themselves to freedom when you left
ironically, though, you were right
life's been good to me while you've been gone
and I've been happy

you can miss them
and still choose
not to go back

you can love them
with your whole heart
and still choose to
prioritize your peace

We grow up watching fairy tales and love stories. We grow up listening to love songs and reading romance novels. Subconsciously, we grow up needing a grand love gesture in order to prove that others love us. But big, grand, true, soulmate love can be found in the smallest details. Love exists in minutiae moments—like ordering two coffees instead of one, like picking the smallest flower on a walk together, like making a homemade pizza instead of ordering one. Love exists through the cracks during the hard times, in the understanding when they're late to events, and in the laughs in car rides when you take wrong turns. It exists in saying sorry, and it exists in forgiveness. Love rarely comes in the form of big moments on television or grand gestures in books. It rarely comes as kisses or dances in the rain or candlelit dinners. It comes every day as steady, consistent, dedicated, and tender gestures. It's something that makes us feel less alone, and it's amazing.

I used to tell myself
that I wasn't deserving
of a love that needs you more
than you need them
that there had to be
something wrong with me
because no one in the world
could fail at love
this many times

I love you, I just can't stay
is what the game would be

and it wasn't until I had lost
an immeasurable amount of times
that I realized
sometimes love is meant to be fleeting
it teaches you that you are not
simply just another heart
to get to know

sometimes love leaves
to teach us how to stay
and get to know
ourselves

I didn't grow simply from age
I grew from the heartbreaks
and trauma
that came after them

I hope you always remember that you never needed anyone else to complete you. Everything that you've been searching for can be found within you. So, if you're out there trying to be loved by someone who'd rather love everything and everyone else around you, just know that the very fact that you're able to give love wholly and completely is what sets you apart from them. You don't need them. You're complete on your own.

losing them is going to hurt and
letting them go is going to hurt like hell
and the sad truth is
you're going to miss them
but the thing is
you can't keep losing yourself
trying to hold on to them
you can't keep making yourself
feel like nothing
trying to make them feel
like they're everything
so let them go
you're going to miss them
and it'll hurt like hell
but through heartbreak
and brokenness
you find yourself

you were never truly broken
even though you felt used
and isolated
and like nothing
would ever fill the emptiness
they left
you knew you were holding on to something
that was holding you back
you don't need others to save you, and
you don't need the person
who made you feel broken
to complete you

I remember wanting to make it work out so badly that I was okay with giving you the world—my world. I was okay with giving you my everything, only to be met with unrequited feelings and disappointment. And even though I gave you so much, you don't owe me anything. You didn't reciprocate the same feelings because you didn't feel the same way. And in the end, it was me who needed to wake up and let you go.

When they come back, and they usually always do, it'll be when you're busy enjoying your life. When you've finally decided to let go and move on, they'll come. And when they do, don't forget how they left. They left without any hesitation, any warning. They left you brokenhearted and questioning your worth. They left you despising the idea of love and terrified of finding it in another relationship. It'll be easy to get caught up in the addiction of them, but don't forget the things that are meant for us are joyous and beautiful, not emotionally excruciating.

You don't need the conversation you think you have to have with them. You'll just end up choosing chemistry over character, and you don't deserve something that unclear, undecided, and gone.

maybe the emptiness you feel
when you close your eyes at night
has been placed there by your own doing

maybe the walls you have constructed
around the hurt
has forged a dam between growth and pain
and you've been stuck in pain
consequently, feeling failure
at the mere touch of a fingertip

I say this because I see you

I see your fingers shaking
heart trembling
at the sight of vulnerability
I see you glancing at the clock
silently wishing to speed time
I see you trying
with all your power
to stay invincible
but have you ever asked yourself
what it would feel like
what would happen
if you were to ever
give in to it all
~stay vulnerable

You thought what the two of you had was perfect. Thought they were *the one* because of the instant connection. You could feel the electricity between you two—feel the need for them in your life like they were water. Maybe it was love, or maybe it was lust; whichever, it was enough for you. The promise of their love was enough. But you shouldn't just live in a world where their love is promised to you. You should live in a world where it's shown to you, every day. Where they take your hand, and they kiss your forehead, and they tell you that nothing in this world would ever make them change the way that they feel about you—the way that they love you, for you. You should live in a world of their love, not just the promise of it.

Right now, you're at a point in your life when you have to make peace a priority. Negativity and romanticizing the past can no longer exist, meaning that you must let go of the people who keep you at arm's length. And even though you desperately wish for them to come back, there will be a time when you're happy they didn't.

if you're strong enough to love them
you're strong enough to walk away
and start a new beginning

at the end of the day
the question isn't *is it enough for them?*
it's *is it enough for you?*
is the constant cycle of running
back into familiar arms and
the looming hope that
there's still something there
ever going to be enough for you?
have you ever thought
that maybe if you say
"enough is enough"
and let them go
you'd finally
be at peace?

you can't keep what's not yours
no matter how heartbreaking the goodbye was
you're brave for letting go of someone
who doesn't want to be held

all I ever wanted was to be enough for you
to know a love
I didn't have to fight for
to hurt for
I never wanted anything from you
that you didn't want to give me on your own
because
I'm not here to fight for anyone to love me
or to be treated right

I wanted to hate you
for the pain that came with trying
to unlove you
for the anxiety-ridden days
that turned into months
trying to wean myself off your memory
and while I was going through hell
trying to move on
you were able to continue living your life
as if nothing happened
I may never get the apology
I know I deserve
but I found closure in knowing
that a love you have to force
is a love that was never meant to be

give yourself the apology
you seek from them
because in the end
it'll be worth more
than what they could
ever offer you

I think the real reason why
it's so hard to let go
why it takes so long
is because you still have hope
and when you've loved someone
unconditionally
for so long
it doesn't really end
no matter how many times
you tell yourself
that it's really over
for you
in your heart
it isn't
but remember
no matter how much
you love them
no matter how hard you try
you can never make
the wrong person
the right person for you

my life changed when I learned
that I wasn't missing what I had with you
I was missing what I never had with you
and now
you're just a lesson that I will always remember

so, it's hard for you to trust
you keep everyone at arm's length
just waiting for the next heartbreak
but it's possible you know
to look at someone and feel like you're home
to feel safe and completely yourself
it was never about finding someone who was perfect
but about finding a place where your flaws are accepted
and your experiences are appreciated
for nothing more than the fact
that they make you
you

I used to be so afraid to be alone
I used to think that
it would make me unlovable
and I think that was the part
of me that made forgetting you
so damn unachievable
but that was never true
and being alone taught me that
loving you was the loneliest
I've ever been

knowing that
where you're going
with or without this person
alone or in love
that's where you're meant to be
that feeling is freeing

realizing that letting someone go
isn't meant to break you
but to build you
that's when you finally start to move on

it was never about seeking and praying for the apology
I thought I needed from you in order to let go
it was about finally finding peace in the apology
I could give myself and
walking away from the people who were unsure of me
no matter how right it felt at the time
no matter how much I wanted them to be my soulmate
sometimes the most beautiful lessons are the hardest
they're the ones that teach you what you deserve

I hope you never feel afraid to let go
I hope you never feel terrified of how big your dreams are
I hope you embrace what the power of healing can do to
you
you deserve to find out who you truly are
you deserve to honor that person
so, it's okay to let go
it's okay to move on to the next big thing in your life
because that next big thing
could be what sets your soul on fire

Finding closure from the broken promises and shattered images from the people who meant the most to you was never about willing yourself not to care about them anymore. It was about finding strength within yourself to let go of the idea of what it could have been. It was about finding a place where you could finally feel safe enough to feel what you really feel, without romanticizing the stories that define where you are now. Because after you mourn what you lost, you end up changing your story. Sometimes the closure you didn't get, was the closure you needed all along. Sometimes it's better not knowing what could have been. You start moving on the day you realize you can't continue revolving around what could have been.

you don't ever have to feel sorry for loving them
for taking a chance on someone who showed you
a glimmer of hope of what love could be
a version of love that you fell in love with
you shouldn't feel ashamed of that
you shouldn't feel like that was a mistake
hell, I think that even makes you brave
life is too damn short
so, you must honor how you show up in this world
you must honor your big heart full of too much love

healing is a choice that's made
because it's a choice that's necessary for growth
don't turn back when it gets hard

focus this time on rediscovering who you are
not why they did what they did
chances are it'll never make sense

do it for you
not for them

it's okay to give yourself permission
to let go of the person you tried to be
to get to know the person you were
too afraid to get to know
the person you were running away from
while you were searching for someone else
because to love yourself means
to let go of those
who don't know how to love
who you are right now

today was an ending
to a story I loved too deeply
and a beginning
to a story I'm just starting to love
it was a goodbye to a life that
brought me happiness and you
but a hello to a journey where
I'm embracing the unknown
with wide arms and a smile
where I'm learning to love me
before I love others

I don't know if this feeling will last forever
if it's just the change in the weather
and tomorrow I'll be right back where I started
but I'm trying
to hold on to this hope
that one day
it'll make sense again
my life will have a purpose and
the memories won't seem so heavy
every day, I wake up
look to the sky
and my wish remains the same
to live a life I'm proud of
and
to love a friend who loves me

the past is not something
that defines who you are now

Love isn't something you have to convince yourself or others to give. It's not something you have to prove that you're enough for—it's something that you choose. Love is something you work toward every day. It's not something you search for in others. It's something that you find within yourself. No amount of time or self-sacrifices will ever convince others to love you. If they can't see that you are someone who's worthy to be loved right now, they never will.

you can't force yourself
to find love and
you can't go looking for it
because if you do
it'll never come to you
take this time to get to know you
and let the blessings fall
into your life

I knew I had to let you go when I saw that I was changing parts of myself so that you'd finally choose me one day. I'm not interested in changing. I'm not interested in maneuvering pieces of myself so that you'd be more invested in a love that I thought we had both felt from the beginning. Love isn't meant to break your heart every day. It's not meant to make you feel unworthy or unloved. Healing happens when you start accepting no less than what you deserve, and I don't deserve a love that compromises the love I have for myself.

I didn't unlove you overnight. I couldn't. Because at a time when everything was dark, I saw a light in you. You reminded me that life was still worth living and that there is still kindness that exists in this world. You made me look forward to something brighter. You made me believe that the right people come into your life at the right time—people who will make you feel every nerve and break in your heart. No, I didn't unlove you overnight. I unloved you in bits and pieces, in laughs and tears . . . over time.

I've stopped settling for indecisive love—for people who are only willing to love with half their heart. The half they haven't already given out to someone else. I'm not interested in giving someone a second chance when they didn't see that I was enough the first time. Because the truth is, you'll never be enough for someone who doesn't see your worth. You'll never be enough for someone who doesn't want to love you right the first time. You deserve someone who can't get enough of you.

Kayla McCullough

I think I'm finally ready to let you go
finally ready to accept that these scars
on my heart came from somewhere
battle wounds from loving too deeply
a reminder of what happens when you fight
for others more than you fight for yourself
they're not something that defines me
but they are a part of me
and for the first time
in a long time
I'm okay with that

"tell me a story"
asked my youngest sister
as I laid her to sleep

"what kind of story do you want to hear?"

"something with a princess"

and while I know
that I will never wear
a glass slipper or
live in a castle
I began to tell her a story

a story of a girl who would overcome
every impossible obstacle
life would throw her way

a girl who would rise
above conditioned expectations
heal herself through
unexpected heartbreak
and still
live a life full of love

I told her a story
of a glass heart

dear reader,

this book starts with the ache that heartache brings,
because that's where my heart was when I first began
writing.

throughout the process of placing my emotions on paper,
I discovered I was healing with every word. the course of
this book has many ups and downs, much like the healing
journey itself, and I thought it necessary to showcase
the progression of that journey within the human body.
your healing will move throughout, and eventually the
ache will dull. I promise you, as time moves, the pain
will eventually lighten, just as this book showcased. I
hope reading this book creates a safe place for you to
experience that pain, just as writing it did for me.

all my love,
kayla

about the author

Kayla McCullough is a poetess and writer residing in the United States.

As a young child, Kayla would often lose herself in books as a way of escapism from real-world experiences. As she grew older, her passion for writing helped her discover who she was, and she began to use poetry to express her thoughts and feelings. She believes that everyone has a story to tell and hopes that her heartfelt poetry encourages readers to share their stories in their own unique ways.

For Kayla, she began reading and sharing her poetry on social media in October of 2021 and has since built a supportive and loving community of readers who encourage her daily to keep telling her story. Known by her fans, friends, and family as a woman who loves a little too much, thinks a little too loudly, and feels a little too deeply, Kayla is only just getting started sharing her voice with the world.

You can follow her journey on social media:
Instagram @kayla.mccul
Tiktok @kayla.mccul